What ao they call pastors in Germany?

German Shepherds

What kind
of cell phone
did Delilah
use?...
Samson

How long did Cain hate his brother? ... As long as he was Abel to.

Why couldn't Jonah trust the ocean?... He just knew there was something fishy about it.

How do we know Peter was a rich fisherman?... By his net income.

Why didn't Noah ever go fishing?... He only had two worms.

Who was the smartest man in the Bible? ... Abraham. He knew a Lot.

What kind of person was Boaz before he got married? ... Ruthless!

Who was the greatest comedian in the Bible? ... Samson. He brought the house down.

Which servant of God was the worst lawbreaker in the Bible? ... Moses. He broke all 10 commandments at once.

At what time of day was Adam created?... A little before Eve.

Which Bible character had no parents?... Joshua, son of Nun.

Early one morning the husband and wife were arguing over who should get out of the warm bed to make the coffee. Finally, the wife folded her arms and said decidedly, "You have to make the coffee. It's in the Bible!"

The husband was shocked. "Is not! Show me!"

Pulling out her Bible, the wife opened it to one of the New Testament books and declared, "It says right here — HEBREWS!"

What
animal
could Noah
not trust?...
Cheetah

Who was the straightest man in the Bible? ...

Joseph: Pharao made him a ruler

During a Sunday school lesson, a child learned about how God created human beings. The child became especially focused when the teacher explained how Eve was created from Adam's ribs. Later in the week, the boy's mother saw him lying down on the floor, so she asked him what was wrong. His reply was priceless: "Mom, I have a pain in my side—I think I'm getting a wife."

What was Moses' wife, Zipphora, known as when she'd throw dinner parties? "The hostess with the Moses."

A little girl finally got to attend a wedding for the first time. While in the church, the girl asked her mother: "Why is the bride dressed in white?" The mother replied to the girl: "because white is the color of happiness and it's the happiest day of her life today."

After a little bit, the girl looks up at her mother and says: "But, then why is the groom wearing black?"

What did the classmate say when asked why they kept walking next to the same person at school? "I was told I'm supposed to walk by Faith!"

Which Bible character was super-fit? Absalom.

What did Adam say when he was asked his favorite holiday? "It's Christmas, Eve."

What did pirates call Noah's boat? "The arrrrrrk."

After service, a stranger approached the pastor and said, "I'd like you to pray for my hearing."

The pastor placed his hands on the man's ears and said a passionate, earnest prayer.

"How's your hearing now?" the pastor asked.

Looking surprised, the man said, "Well, it's not until tomorrow."

How are toddlers and those who attempted to build a tower to Heaven similar? They all babble.

After the wedding, the little ringbearer asked his father, "How many brides can the groom marry?"

"One," his father said. "Why do you ask?"

"Because the priest said he could marry sixteen," the boy said, puzzled.

"How'd you come up with that?" his father asked.

"Easy," the little boy said. "All you have to do is add it up like the priest said: 4 better, 4 worse, 4 richer, 4 poorer."

Why didn't anyone want to fight Goliath? It seemed like a giant ordeal.

Which king liked to do things on his own? Solomon

Why did Adam and Eve do math every day? They were told to be fruitful and multiply.

What did Daniel tell his real estate agent? "I'd prefer a house with no den."

How did
Joseph
make his
coffee?
Hebrewed it.

What's loved by Noah and also most meat-eaters? Ham.

How do you know Pharaoh was athletic? He had a court.

When someone needed a boat made, what did the people in town say? "We Noah guy.

What did Zachariah do when he and Elizabeth had disagreements? He gave the silent treatment.

What's a miracle that can be done by a complainer? Turning anything into whine.

How do pastors like their orange juice? With pulpit.

Who was the fastest runner in the race?

Adam. He was first in the human race.

Why didn't they play cards on the Ark? Because Noah was always standing on the deck

Did Eve ever have a date with Adam? Nope — just an apple.

Why did the unemployed man get excited while reading his Bible?

He thought he saw a job.

What's so funny about forbidden fruits? They create many jams.

Who was the first tennis player in the bible?

Joseph because he served in Pharaoh's court

Who is the greatest babysitter mentioned in the Bible?
David — he rocked Goliath to a very deep sleep

How do groups of angels greet each other? Halo, halo, halo!

What do we have that Adam never had?

Ancestors.

Who do
mice
pray to?
Cheesus.

Why did Noah have to punish and discipline the chickens on the Ark?
They were using fowl language.

Who was the best female finance lady in the Bible? Pharaoh's daughter. She went down to the bank of the Nile and drew out a little prophet

Which Bible Character is a locksmith? Zaccheus.

What's the best way to study the Bible? You Luke into it.

What do you call a priest who becomes a lawyer? A father-in-law.

Why did the sponge go to church?

It was hole-y.

What did God do to cure Moses' headache? He gave him two tablets.

What did Moses say when he saw people worshipping the golden calf?
Holy cow!

Where is the best place to get an ice cream cone? Sunday School.

What is a mathematician's favorite book of the Bible? Numbers.

What type of lights did Noah have on the Ark? Floodlights.

Why did Samson try to avoid arguing with Delilah? He didn't want to split hairs.

Which area of the Promised Land was especially wealthy?

The area around the Jordan where the banks kept overflowing.

Why wouldn't the Pharaoh let the Hebrews go?
He was in 'de Nile.

What is a salesman's favorite Scripture passage? The Great Commission.

What is a missionary's favorite kind of car?

A convertible.

Why is Swiss considered the most religious type of cheese?
It's hole-y.

What is a dentist's favorite hymn? Crown him with many crowns.

Why did Moses cross the Red Sea?
To get to the other side.

Why is it that Jesus cannot wear necklaces? Because He is the one who breaks every chain.

What is the court's favourite Bible book? Judges

Both a priest and a taxi driver died and were resurrected. St. Peter was waiting for them at the Pearly Gates. St. Peter motioned to the taxi driver, 'Come with me.' The taxi driver followed St Peter to a mansion as instructed. It had everything imaginable, from a bowling alley to an Olympic-sized pool. 'Oh my word, thank you,' the taxi driver said. St. Peter then led the priest to a run-down shack with a bunk bed and an old television set. 'Wait, I think you're a little confused,' the priest said. 'Shouldn't it be me who gets the mansion?' After all, I was a priest who went to church every day and preached the word of God.' 'That is correct.' 'But during your sermons, people slept,' St Peter countered. Everyone prayed as the taxi driver drove

What did God say after He created Adam? "I can do better than that." And so, He created woman.

If Goliath would come back to life today, would you like to tell him the joke about David and Goliath?
No, he already fell for it once.

Don't let your worries get the best of you. Remember, Moses started out as a basket case.

Mrs. Smartt was fumbling in her purse for her offering when a large television remote fell out and clattered into the aisle. The curious usher bent over to retrieve it for her and whispered, "Do you always carry your TV remote to church?"

"No," she replied, "but my husband refused to come with me this morning, and I figured this was the most evil thing I could do to him legally."

My sister
only believes
in 20% of
the bible.
She's an
eight-theist.

Why don't pastors ever play hide and seek? Because they always want to be found in God's presence!

What kind of car did the disciples drive? A Honda, because they were all in one accord!

Why did the church choir start a gardening club? Because they wanted to "grow" in faith!

What's the best day to go to the beach? Psalm Sunday!

Why did the scarecrow become a successful preacher? Because he was outstanding in his field!

What did the grape say when it got stepped on during communion? Nothing, it just let out a little wine!

Why did the pastor bring a pencil to the sermon? In case he needed to draw people closer to God!

Why don't Christians ever get locked out of church? Because Jesus is the key!

What did the preacher say at the salad bar? "Lettuce pray!"

Why did the Christian athlete go to church? To get some "prayer-formance" tips!

What do you call a church meeting at the beach? A "sand-tuary"!

What do you call a Christian cow? A "holy" cow!

Why did the bicycle fall over at church? Because it was two-tired!

Why did the Christian musician start a gardening business? Because he wanted to plant seeds of faith!

How do you make holy water for a baptism? You boil the hell out of it!

Why was the pastor so good at fishing? Because he had a "divine" hook!

What do you call a belt made out of Bibles? Scripture-tight!

What do you call a cow that just gave birth at church? A "moo-ther" of God!

Why did the Christian comedian always bring a Bible to his shows? Because he wanted to "testify" to good humor!

Why was the church so bright at night?
Because it had a "light" that never went out!

Why did the preacher always have snacks during the sermon? Because he wanted to "feed" the flock!

Why did Jesus make so much bread and fish? Because He wanted to "take-away" the hunger of the crowd!

"Once, a church member fell asleep during my sermon. After the service, I asked him, 'Was the sermon that bad?' He replied, 'No, Pastor, it was so good, I wanted to hear it again in my dreams!'"

"I heard about a talking dog who came to church last Sunday. I asked him, 'What did you think of the sermon?' He replied, 'Rough!'"

"I met a hiker who said he feels closest to God when he's on a mountain. I told him, 'That's because you're on a 'high'er ground!'"

"Why did the chef become a Christian? Because he wanted to 'taste and see' that the Lord is good!"

"Why did the fisherman join the church choir? Because he wanted to 'catch' the spirit!"

"Why did the baker bring doughnuts to the church? Because he wanted to 'glaze' the path to salvation!"

Made in United States
Troutdale, OR
10/18/2023